YOU CAN KNOW IT'S TRUE LOVE

JOHN M. DRESCHER

Wipf & Stock
PUBLISHERS
Eugene, Oregon

Wipf and Stock Publishers
199 W 8th Ave, Suite 3
Eugene, OR 97401

You Can Know It's True Love
By Drescher, John M.

ISBN: 1-57910-102-X
Publication date 7/8/2002
Previously published by Baker Book House, 1983

A young college couple came to my office the other day to talk about their relationship. "We want to know," they said, "whether ours is real love or not. We are not sure at times if what we have going is enough for us to continue together. How can we know if our love is real enough for marriage? How can we know what true love is?"

My office is on a college campus. I speak to college students in the Sunday morning service. Early each year I schedule a series of speeches on love, sex, and marriage. As a result students come for counsel, and I find a rather new thing happening among young people. Many youth today are seeking out counsel when they sense their relationship may be serious enough to think of engagement and marriage, yet before they become engaged. At this point they feel hesitant. Not only do they have fears in light of all of today's marriage failures, but also they are mature enough to realize that more is required to make a marriage work than the infatuation of earlier years.

This is good. It is better to look at what true love means and know how to test true love before becoming too seriously involved. True love can stand scrutiny and testing. When one is hesitant to have a relationship tested it is not yet of the right fiber or material to make a durable marriage.

The Meaning of Love

William Barclay of Scotland says that if a lad loves a lass the Gaelic language has twenty different ways to tell her so. The English language limits us in the expression of love. Today the word *love* means too many things and serves too many purposes. It can mean the love of God for us or our love for God. It can refer to the superficial love of one taking his fourth wife, or it can describe what happens when a mother gives her life for a child. So our English word is woefully inadequate.

Then again definitions of love leave us cold. How do you describe an experience like love? It may be of some help to review different words for love.

In the Greek language there are four words for love. To understand true love all four words must be incorporated into a full definition.

Eros—Getting Love

First there is *eros*. There is a getting love. It is the Greek word from which we get our word *erotic*. It is a changeable love; it depends on the response of another. *Eros* refers primarily to the physical side of love—the response to beauty, charm, ability, lovableness, pleasure, and sexual appeal. It includes all loving physical experiences of maleness and femaleness which add intimacy to a relationship from the touch of the fingers, a back rub, the loving look or kiss, to sexual intercourse. It speaks of physical attraction and attachment.

Eros is love because of the lovability of another. The basic element is desire or pleasure in another for the completion of one's own joy, pleasure, or satisfaction.

As always, the temptation is to pervert, to take that which is for our happiness and use it to our destruction. So *eros* can be shallow and self-centered. *Eros* can be selfish and turned inward. Then it becomes brittle and breaks. When it is self-centered it subsequently becomes self-destructive. It can simply mean that as long as the other deserves my love, desires my love, exalts me, gives what I want, I will love. But if the lovable one ceases to respond or deserve it in my way, *eros* is killed.

Stergo—Caring Love

A second Greek word which can help us in our understanding of the meaning of love is *stergo*. This is a caring love. It is the natural and normal love which we have for others as part of the human race. *Stergo* is the recognition that we are interdependent and interrelated people. We have deep feelings of being closely bound together. We have an obligation to each other. It is the natural love of humans concerned about what happens to other humans because of a common kinship in creation.

We hurt when others suffer; we rejoice when others rejoice. We give when there is need.

Philia—Sharing Love

A third word which can help us to understand the largeness of love is the word *philia*. This is a sharing love. In a good marriage a loving husband and wife are more than lovers. They are also good friends. They have affection for each other. Their love is based on many common interests, activities, concerns, and desires.

Philia means companionship and communication. It means to crave each other's company. It is not the love of passion but the love of partnership which the Scripture refers to in saying, "It is not good . . . to be alone" (Gen. 2:18). *Philia* is love, not of physical touch but of togetherness, not of competition so much as cooperation to which the Scripture speaks in Genesis 2:18b, "I will make a helper . . . for him." It is the love of Titus 2:4 where the older women are urged to teach the younger women to love (be affectionate) to their husbands.

While *eros* is more a face-to-face relationship, *philia* is more a shoulder-to-shoulder relationship. This love finds its oneness in a common cause which is greater than one can assume alone. It includes the cooperation in anything from eating breakfast and doing the dishes together to praying and playing together to serving others together in many ways. *Philia* is the love, not of looking into each other's eyes, but of joining each other's hands in all of life together.

Agape—Giving Love

A fourth essential love in human relationships is *agape*. This is giving love. It is the pure, outgoing desire to care for and bless the other. It does not give with the expectation of return. It gives when the other is not able to reciprocate. So it continues to carry on through sickness, failure, and difficulty. *Agape* does not do away with *eros, stergo,* or *philia*; but it controls all for the best and seeks the highest fulfillment for the one loved. A very practical definition of love is given by psychiatrist Harry Stack Sullivan: "When the satisfaction or the security of another person becomes as significant to one as one's own satisfaction or security, then the state of love exists." While this is an insightful definition, Christian love goes beyond this.

Agape includes surrender, self-sacrifice, and self-giving which puts the loved one first and seeks the happiness of the other before its own. It gives gladly, rather than seeking to get, only to find out that it usually gains more than it gives.

A Paean of Love

Henry Drummond described *agape* in I Corinthians 13 as a spectrum of nine hues. This love is defined by what it does and does not do. Notice the many hues of love.

1. *Love is patient.* True love bears up under stress. It can wait. Patience is the power to see things through. It speaks of the willingness to defer judgment. And it does not lose hope in another. Love bears the everyday trials and annoyances of life quietly and calmly.

2. *Love is kind.* Kindness is love in little things. It is love in action. Joseph Joulert wrote, "A part of kindness consists in loving people more than they deserve." Kindness gives a helping hand and a healing touch in time of trouble. Roy O. McClain says, "When I look back on my own paltry life the things that stand out are few. Not the publicity, the degrees, not the facts memorized. The only things that stand out are the few things in which I have tried to be kind."

3. *Love envies not.* This love is not in competition with others. Envy is feeling bad when someone else has excelled, particularly in the same area of work or expertise. Love enjoys the success of another and does not detract by word or action from the status of another.

4. *Love is not boastful.* The one who loves another does not brag of his own accomplishments. There is a profound humility in love and a promoting of the other's accomplishments.

5. *Love is courteous.* Love is sensitive to little things and small concerns. Nothing in another's life is inconsequential to love's concern. Love is courteous because it cares and values others.

6. *Love does not seek its own.* Selfishness and love are opposites. Love fulfills itself by giving itself. Love does not talk about sticking up for its rights. Love's concerns is the other's right.

7. *Love is not irritable.* It is not touchy. Self is touchy. Love sweetens life by kind words in the face of conflict and loving acts in the face of abrasiveness.

8. *Love does not think evil.* Love is not suspicious and does not imagine the worst on the part of another's actions or speech. Rather love puts on the best connotations. It trusts and believes the best.

9. *Love rejoices, not in wrong but in the truth.* It takes no pleasure in evil reports or gossip, no matter who is involved. Love cannot rejoice in evil, but it rejoices when the good triumphs.

What is love? Look again at what love does, how it responds, and its characteristics. Notice this nine-point paean of love. It shall forever be the clearest definition of love.

"Remember that love is not getting but giving," exclaims Henry Van Dyke, "not a wild dream of pleasure and a madness of desire—oh, no, love is not that; and it is the best thing in the world and the thing that lives longest."

The Myths of Love

Many myths about love are afloat. We can better understand the characteristics of real love by looking at some of the persisting myths. Listing them should put us on guard.

Love at First Sight

Let us first state that there is no such thing as love at first sight. One may be attracted to another at first sight, but love grows by mutual esteem and appreciation, and all growth takes time. One does not fall in love; one grows in love. A boy may be attracted to the way a girl walks and a girl may be excited by his attention to her, but that is not love. Certainly this kind of attraction might develop into a lasting affection, but for that to happen it will take time—lots of time seeing the other in all kinds of situations, under many different circumstances.

Attraction is possible without a knowledge of the other's traits, personality, or character, but love is a process of growth and development, and there is nothing automatic about it. This is why studies show clearly that persons who have dated at least two years have a much better chance for a happy marriage.

The love-at-first-sight myth also carries the idea that when love hits you, you will know it because it will sweep you off your feet, suddenly, without warning. Love at first sight may be merely a couple's need finding expression in a romantic attachment. It is a form of sheer sentimentality, fed by all the romantic illusions propagated by films, TV, and love stories. It is being in love with love rather than in love with the realities of life.

During courtship many times people, young and old, tend to lose their sense of judgment. Nature makes men and women so attractive to each other that they don't stop to consider whether they have any other qualifications for making a life together.

Love Will Solve All

Another myth of love, which develops an unreal or unhealthy attachment to another, is characterized by the feeling that love will solve all problems. Those who believe this myth are impatient with any interruption or interference or questions about the relationship or about postponing desires.

In spite of clear conflicts and points of incompatibility, the love-solves-all attitude ignores reality to live in a dream world of unreality. It believes that annoying habits and selfishness will be done away with after marriage. Love will reform the drunk, the promiscuous, the one who can't hold a job. It will make an immature person into a mature adult.

As someone points out, marrying a total abstainer won't cure an alcoholic any more than marrying a musician will give a deaf person absolute pitch. And people who marry each other so they will stop being lonely discover the most excruciating loneliness of all, the kind shared with another. Some of the loneliest people alive are married people. Love will provide motivation to work toward solutions, but love will not make an unwise spender into a skillful buyer. We don't marry to solve our problems.

> One of the most dangerous assumptions about love is the idea that two persons who are in love should marry because they are in love. Evidently we have never been told that it is quite possible to fall in love with a person with whom we cannot have a successful marriage. We do not know that some people who get divorced are still in love with each other. Romance is not possible in a marriage where there is no love: on the other hand, romance may disappear quickly from that marriage when people assumed that love was all that was necessary and could be trusted as the only guide into marriage.[1]

A love-solves-all approach is pure deception and leads to complete disillusionment. This myth leads people to look at only a few characteristics of the other person instead of appraising the total personality. It refuses to look at and to weigh those traits of personality which are problem areas.

True love dares to ask questions and opens

1. W. Clark Ellzey, "How to Keep Romance in Your Marriage" (Associated Press), p. 21.

itself to analysis. It risks comparisons and wants to know the truth. True love faces reality.

Love Is a Feeling

Beware of the myth that love is a feeling, because it is sure to disappoint soon under the pressures of daily living. A relationship which depends on feelings will have little real love in the long run. There are those who think they love because they feel so good. They are in love with a feeling of love without really loving. This level of love is one of the reasons for all the petty jealousies of adolescents and other immature persons.

Mothers do not get up in the middle of the night to feed a crying baby because they have a good feeling when they get up at midnight. They get up because they love. Love has deeper roots than mere feelings. Love is a sense of deep respect, appreciation, and concern for another. Love is dedication and devotion. If a family or couple does good acts and expresses love only when feeling especially loving, little love will be expressed in the long run.

As long as love is confined to feelings only, it is self-centered and continually asks, "What do I get out of this relationship?" It cannot carry persons through the difficulties of marriage and family.

So the philosophy of "we will live together as long as we love" is doomed from the start. This idea, which became popular in recent years, is based on feeling. "To love someone," says Erich Fromm, "is not just a strong feeling. It is a decision, it is a judgment, it is a promise."[2] C. S. Lewis says that we sign a contract when we marry because we realize that there will be times of conflict, boredom, and monotony. Therefore, we pledge our word to one another, before others, saying, "I take you for better or for worse, for richer or for poorer, in sickness as in health, till death do us part." We are saying, "You can depend upon me to stick with you, and I'll not walk out on you no matter what."

I was speaking on marriage to a large group of youths. Noting the expressions on their faces and a few whispers between several of them I stopped and asked them what they were thinking. They responded, "But we will never do it like our parents. We will never marry for as long as we live; we will marry for as long as we love." My immediate response was that such a marriage will not last long, because in every marriage there are those difficulties which cause the greatest lovers to doubt their love. Love is not just a feeling. Love is a commitment.

> An individual can actually love being loved, or love the feeling of being loved, or even love the feeling of loving—and yet not be in love. . . .

2. Erich Fromm, *The Art of Loving* (New York: Harper and Row, 1974), p. 56.

> Sometimes a person has a strong urge to love another, and this urge focuses upon the first one of the opposite sex who is normally attractive and who responds with a little affection. It is a form of sheer sentimentality, fed by all of the romantic illustrations propagated by our culture.[3]

Love Is Blind

An old adage says, "Love is blind," and therein lies a great truth and great untruth. It is true that true love overlooks many faults. However, those greatly infatuated idealize each other. Such see only perfection and are blinded to human frailties, foibles, and follies. Herein lies the danger of this myth because this kind of blindness can end in painful discovery.

Love that lasts is not blind. It has enough realism to see each other clearly enough so that further acquaintance is a pleasant adventure. This again is the reason why lasting love is based on long acquaintance. For love to grow it must see. A good test of love is whether or not two persons grow more and more fond of each other as time goes on and as they see each other under all kinds of circumstances—happy and unhappy, delightful and disappointing.

A lasting love is real because it is based on recognized realities. Each finds the other lov-

3. Dwight H. Small, *Design for Christian Marriage* (Old Tappan, N.J.: Revell, 1959), p. 116.

able through actual experience and not only in a dream world.

Love Is Physical

With physical maturity comes deep feelings of physical attraction. The desire to be close, to touch, and to possess can be so strong as to be perplexing. These surging, sex-toned emotions are so powerful and so insistent they may be confused with real love. So it is good to remember that sexual attraction is normal and right, but it is only one facet of love. It dare not control or override other important facets needed for a good relationship. Sex is an important and good part of marriage, but it is only one segment of marriage and is reserved for marriage.

One of the tricks of love is to imagine that strong physical attraction is love. In his excellent book *Love and Sex Are Not Enough*, Charles DeSanta points out that it is possible to feel the urgent tug of sex appeal for someone with whom you would not and should not build a happy long-term relationship.

This romantic lie says in one way or another, that love is proven or even tested by sex outside of marriage. There are all kinds of arguments for premarital sex because anyone who goes beyond what is considered right needs reasons. So the argument on compatibility is used. "How else can you discover your compatibility?" Others propose that "love makes it right." Still others reason that "the sexually experienced are better prepared for marriage."

These arguments, along with any other argument for premarital sex, are very spurious because none of them are true. Much more can be learned about compatibility through becoming acquainted as persons on many other levels than through sexual familiarity which has a way of stifling other levels of learning. Sexual relationships are certainly not right without love, but if love makes everything right there will be little faithfulness before or after marriage because there will be many loves during a lifetime. And why do those who engage in premarital sex so many times insist on finding a virgin to marry if sexual experience prepares for marriage?

> Acquisitive, possessive love always fails to win another's love, or even respect. This is the theory that many people cannot understand. When you say, "prove your love for me by doing what I want," you are using your love as a whip and it will be deeply resented and resisted. You are treating me as an "it" to be used, manipulated, acquired.[4]

Where real love exists persons are protective and tender toward each other. They want to

4. Lance Webb, *Discovering Love* (Nashville: Abingdon, 1959), p. 41.

safeguard what is beautiful and sacred in their love. And when anyone wants to test love by engaging in premarital sex it is good to ask, "If you really love me why do you want me to do that which I believe to be wrong and which could have serious lifelong consequences?" One who loves never exploits the beloved. Selfishness and a desire for personal gratification are not love. Part of the romantic lie is that if people are compatible sexually there is harmony and happiness.

In his fine book *So You Are Going to Be Married,* Dr. Clair Amstutz, says:

> Finally, the conviction has been slowly growing that the spiritual aspects of marriage are more important than the biological ones. This idea came slowly because all American literature on marriage has stressed the physical with emphasis on anatomy and physiology, and that was my particular training. . . . I thought I was making an original discovery when I saw that those who have great spiritual resources generally have no problem of "incompatibility."[5]

Infatuation Versus Love

Help may be found in understanding love by quickly contrasting true love and infatuation. Infatuation is an unreasonable, sentimental, or

5. Clair Amstutz, *So You're Going to Be Married* (Scottdale, Pa.: Herald Press, 1971), pp. 6-7.

unhealthy attachment. Infatuation may happen suddenly while love grows. Infatuation is easily recognized because it usually sweeps people off their feet. Love grows as persons share all kinds of activities and ideas and experiences. Infatuation usually comes suddenly after a date or two and effects little change in the relationship as time goes on.

Infatuation is self-centered and is most concerned about "I" and "me" and "mine," while love is selfless in its desire to protect the other and to do things for the other which bring happiness. Love is a "we" think, "we" do, "we" like, "we" go, and "we" plan identification and bond.

Infatuation usually takes only one or at best a few characteristics of the other into account while love sees more than a few segments of the person. Love seeks to see the whole person while infatuation sees only those traits of the person which are attractive. An infatuated girl can see a tall, handsome athlete and overlook the fact that his way of life would be totally unacceptable with her standards or beliefs. An infatuated boy may see a girl who is a beauty queen but not raise the question, "Would she be the kind of mother I'd want for my children?"

Infatuation tends to be fickle by nature, unable to make up its mind between persons, while love is selective. A person in loves prefers the company of the loved one and is no longer happy to date just anyone.

Infatuation lives with distrust, insecurity, and

jealousy, while love implies trust, security, freedom, and mutual concern. Infatuation is usually a symbol of success and uses a person to build or restore a sense of insecurity. So infatuation involves jealousy and is very insecure if a partner even looks or talks to another. Dwight Small says,

> When one says: "I can't live without you," it is usually infatuation . . . This is not love, but rather a sign of dependency, of a compulsive need for self-assurance, or perhaps of one's sensing that he has not developed the capacity truly to love someone else.[6]

Infatuation tends to disregard or evade decisions. Love seeks to solve problems and reach mature and responsible decisions.

Infatuation makes the physical the center of the relationship while love gives meaning to the physical. Infatuation sees sex out of proportion to the whole relationship. Sex and physical expression take precedence in such a relationship, while love sees physical expressions of love as part of a larger whole.

The Marks of Love

Walter Trobisch suggests six tests for love in his excellent book, *I Married You.*[7] Let me list these and comment briefly on each.

6. Small, *Design for Christian Marriage,* p. 123.

7. Walter Trobisch, *I Married You* (New York: Harper and Row, 1975), pp. 75-77.

The Sharing Test

This one deals with the depth of sharing which you are able to do and is sometimes called the expression test. When you experience something good or read something you enjoy, what is your first thought? Do you have a deep desire to share and discuss it with the one you love? When you do something do you want to do that which will be a shared pleasure? Do you want to share your happiness or do you still seek your own happiness primarily? Do you have a growing longing to share all life together?

Gustave Thibon writes:

> Love is pure when its thirst for happiness gives way to its passion for unity. As long as two beings are joined together by the mere desire for happiness, they are not truly in love. They are still parted. Love is the union of two lives, not two joys.[8]

In a counseling session with an engaged couple the counselor asked them many questions about each other. When he was finished he asked each one, "Were there any surprises?" "Not really," they responded. "Good," he replied. "If you could say all those things about yourselves without surprises to each other it tells me you have passed the sharing test."

I have counseled many couples and one thing

8. Gustave Thibon, *What God Has Joined Together* (Plainfield, N.J.: Logos, 1967), p. 159.

I want to know from such couples is how free they feel in expressing themselves to each other. Love has the ability to discuss differences and by doing so develops deeper appreciation for each other. Love has a deep desire to discuss differences rather than dodge difficulties. Does silence make you uncomfortable in each other's presence? Marriage is made up of many moments of silence. Do you feel free to express yourself? Can you say what you think and still feel accepted and loved? Or do you feel worried about what you said?

Dinah Maria Mulock Craik expresses it this way:

> Oh, the comfort—the inexpressible comfort of
> feeling safe with a person,
> Having neither to weigh thoughts,
> Nor measure words—but pouring them
> All right out—just as they are—
> Chaff and grain together—
> Certain that a faithful hand will
> Take and sift them—
> Keep what is worth keeping—
> And with the breath of kindness
> Blow the rest away.

Is your love one that meets the sharing test?

Sometimes in counseling young people I asked them, "How do you feel after a date?" Some have said, "I feel like a better person." "I feel like a person of more worth." Others have told me, "After a date I worry about having said something in the wrong way." "I go to my room and cry because I'm not sure how I was taken." My response to this is, "How long will you be able to live with that?" A test of true love is the freedom of expression and sharing and the feeling of acceptance in doing so.

The Strength Test

By this test Trobisch refers to how your relationship effects you physically. Real love should not sap strength but give you renewed energy and strength. Love is characterized by joy. Joy and happiness make you more creative and stimulate you to greater and greater accomplishments. I have met young people who, because of the pressures which their daily relationship brings, become more haggard and weakened. Their strength seems drained so that they have difficulty keeping at their jobs or school work. True love has a way of filling life with freshness and freedom. Does your relationship give you new strength and energy or take away your vibrancy and strength?

The Respect Test

In order for a growing relationship of love to develop there must be deep respect for each other. Do you really have respect for each other? Are you proud of your partner in front of your friends and family? Love grows by mutual respect and appreciation. Do you respect the viewpoints of each other? If not there is danger ahead. It is difficult to imagine a happy marriage when respect is absent. When you respect each other you make each other respectable. When you honor each other you make each other honorable. When you see each other as beautiful you beautify each other's lives. Love confirms and builds self-respect.

Do you have the respect for each other which will build a stronger and stronger relationship? Do you feel proud to be with the loved person in the presence of all the people you know?

The Habit Test

All of us have habits and traits which can be very annoying. You dare not think that these annoyances will disappear automatically after marriage. Although it is true that love overlooks faults, these have a way of magnifying themselves in the constant companionship of marriage. Are you able to accept and appreciate each other in spite of habits and shortcomings? You marry an entire person and your love must be large enough to overlook faults and even enjoy and like the special differences each brings to marriage. As long as you are out to work each other over, you are headed for heartache and your love is not large enough to endure. I think of a couple whom I've always admired. They are far from perfect, yet I've always enjoyed seeing how they delight in each other's differences, even their oddities.

Do you love to accept each other with all your habits and shortcomings? As you look over the history of your relationship have you grown in fondness, in contagion for each other, and in appreciation of each other's differences?

The Quarrel Test

Dr. Trobisch says,

> When a couple comes to me and wants to get married, I always ask them if they have had a real quarrel—not just a casual difference of opinion, but a real fight.
>
> Many times they will say, "Oh, No! pastor, we love each other!"
>
> Then I will tell them: "Quarrel first, then I will marry you."
>
> The point is, of course, not the quarrel, but the ability to be reconciled to each other. This ability must be trained and tested before marriage. Not sex, but rather the quarrel test is a "required" pre-marital experience.[9]

So, how do you feel after an argument? Are you bittered and soured or do you have a mutual let's-talk-it-all-out agreement, followed by a deep sense of appreciation? If you can't ride out differences or arguments with deep love and respect for each other, take another look at yourself and how you relate.

9. Trobisch, *I Married You*, p. 76.

Are you able to give in, compromise, and forgive? Is the love you have together great enough to weather the crises and conflicts and misunderstandings that come as you grow together? The ability to experience loving reconciliation after difference of opinion is a test of true love.

The Time Test

Trobisch quotes an old saying, "Never get married until you have summered and wintered with your partner!" Have you known each other long enough to know each other well enough? Studies are clear that short courtships often result in short marriages. It stands to reason you cannot learn to know the many elements of personality in a short time.

It takes time to see how a person responds under varied circumstances, to test responsibility, and to sense whether a person has the loyalty and love to last a lifetime. It takes time to learn if the person respects others and how the person handles tension and stress.

True love can stand the test of time. Love is not in a hurry. Does your love stand the test of time? Have you applied the test of time?

William J. McRae in his book *Preparing For Marriage* adds additional tests of true love.

The Separation Test

Is the most wonderful thought to be with the loved one and the most unhappy thought to be separated from that person? Do you feel an unusual joy when in the company of each other and an unusual loss when separated?

In counseling college students I have many times used the separation test. Here students see so much of each other and are together so often that they have trouble backing up and looking at themselves and their relationship with all its realities. I suggest they agree to separate for a week or two and sense how they feel. For some the separation firms their deep love; for others it reveals how easily they can get along without each other.

If yours is true love you can mean all the more to each other after separation. And if your love will not stand the test of absence, it will not stand the far more frequent test of presence.

Sometimes young persons will be separated because of service or summer, and it has proved an excellent chance to assess true feelings and to look objectively at their relationship. This is good because true love can stand the separation test. If the love is not genuine it is best to discover so before marriage.

The Giving Test

Love is giving, not getting. Are you in love to give and are you capable of self-giving? Much unhappiness later in life arises out of immaturity which is manifest in the selfishness which says: "If he/she loved me he/she would make me happy!" This is still selfish love which is out to get rather than to give.

It is self-giving love alone, not getting love, which makes life full and rich and satisfying. In mature love, romance is no longer defined by what one receives. Real love is gauged and guided by the needs and the best welfare of the other.

Is your relationship one in which you give freely without thought of return? What is the basis of the attraction? Is it what the person can give you or what you feel you together can give to the relationship?

The Growth Test

Here the test is whether your love is dynamic in its growth. Love enlarges all it touches. Is it making both of you better and bigger persons? Do you help each other to your highest ideals? Are the characteristics of Christian love developing? Do objects and things associated with the loved person have greater meaning because of him or her?

An unknown poet expresses the growth test well.

I love you
Not only for what you are,
But for what I am
When I am with you,

I love you,
Not only for what

You have made of yourself,
But for what
You are making of me.

I love you
For the part of me
That you bring out
I love you
For putting your hand
Into my heaped-up heart
And passing over
All the foolish, weak things
That you can't help
Dimly seeing there,
And for drawing out
Into the light
All the beautiful belonging
That no one else had looked
Quite far enough to find.

I love you because you
Are helping me to make
Of the lumber of my life
Not a tavern
But a temple:
Out of the works
Of every day
Not a reproach
But a song. . . .

The Sex Test

As you consider the question of attraction, can you enjoy being with the loved one without physical sharing and physical expression of your love? Is there a mutual enjoyment of each other without the constant need for physical expression? If you can't be together without petting, you do not have the maturity and love essential for marriage. Sex is important, very important, but it is only one part of love. You sin against the deeper meaning of love if your interest is only physical.

Sex is no test of love. If you want to use sex to test whether you love each other, you should ask, "Do I love so little that I need sex to prove it?"

One final but important word must be added. Love is a large word, a very large word. And true love includes another large word, the word *commitment*. To love in the sense spoken of by this little booklet is to be ready to commit oneself for life even as the Scripture and wedding vows state. It is to live together until death parts.

Elizabeth Barrett Browning expressed love in beautiful words:

> How do I love thee? Let me count the ways:
> I love thee to the depth and breadth and height
> My soul can reach, when feeling out of sight
> For the ends of being and ideal Grace.
> I love thee to the level of everyday's
> Most quiet need, by sun and candlelight.
> I love thee freely, as men strive for Right;
> I love thee purely, as they turn from Praise
> I love thee with the passion put to use

In my old griefs, and with my childhood's faith;
I love thee with a love I seemed to lose
With my lost saints—I love thee with the breath,
Smiles, tears, of all my life! And if God choose,
I shall but love thee better after death.